HUMPHREY'S ADVENTURES
IN KINDERGARTEN

BOOK TWO: The Pumpkin Patch

Written By: Terry Vail Blount

Illustrated By: Jeanne McGaha Munden

I dedicate this book to my TLC Kindergarten class of 1995-1996,
to Carley Cardinal, who always knew the scoop on all of us!
And to my grandchildren who are loved more than words can say.
Terry Vail Blount

This book is dedicated to my granddaughters Blair and Alora.
You are my sunshine!
Jeanne McGaha Munden

Dean K.

Grey F.

Janae' B.

Kaitlin M.

Kendall S.

Logan M.

Mallory J.

Matt B.

Matthew D.

Matt M.

Melissa M.

Morgan K.

Sam D.

Suzie B.

William Q.

Zachary H.

Hello, my name is Humphrey.

I am a dog in case you didn't notice,
but believe me I am no ordinary dog....

Many years ago, my boy and I were best friends,
but he grew up, so his mom, Mrs. B brought me to
school to visit her Kindergarten class and now I get to
go home with a different student each night.

Suzie
Sam

Suzie's name is pulled from the name jar;

I am waiting in my backpack on her coat hook;

here she comes, she is taking me to her car;

and now she buckled our seat belts!

Suzie's mom is our music teacher at TLC;
believe me, we sang many songs while she was driving.

We went to a special place that had a
flashing red light saying the doughnuts were hot.

Suzie, her brother Gregory, and Ms. Denise
sure do like doughnuts and now I know why.

We all enjoyed the yummy doughnuts in the car!

Then Suzie asked her mom to buy some doughnuts
to share at school for tomorrow's snack,
she is so thoughtful.

When we finally arrived at Suzie's house,
she let me know how much she misses her dad
because he has been gone for a long time.

Her dad is in the United States Navy
and he works with a special boat unit
that supports the Navy Seals.

I did not know that seals could be in the Navy.

Ketc
Mus
S
P

We played games,
and we sang more songs;
Suzie sure loves to sing a song
about a big pumpkin.

We ate our dinner "picnic style" on the floor.

Suzie asked her dog Buddy to share
his kibbles with me, and he did!

As we ate, we watched her favorite
show about the ocean;
I think she was looking for those Navy seals.

HUMPHREY

It was time for baths and bed,
we said our prayers and
Ms. Denise read us some books in Suzie's bed.

Then Suzie put some Halloween stickers
in my journal, she is so kind.

When I woke up,
Ms. Denise and Gregory
were asleep in Suzie's bed!

There is a lot of love from this place,
and I feel it!

3 4 5 6 7 8 9 10

Back at school,
the students were working at learning centers.

Listen, the ringing bell means
clean-up and go to circle time.

After doing our morning routine
starting with the pledge,
singing a song about America and
learning about our special letter sounds,
it was finally time for Mrs. B
to read my journal.

However, she did not read it;
Mrs. B told us to get our jackets on
and quietly line up behind our line-leader.

We were going on a field trip on a big bus
and we were going to a farm
that has a pumpkin patch.

It was a long, bumpy bus ride
and I liked it!

When we arrived at the farm
we all hopped onto a wagon pulled by a tractor.

We had another bumpy ride out to the fields
where we saw cows, horses, sheep,
goats, chickens and turkeys.

We all jumped off the wagon
right next to the pumpkin patch.

Mrs. B said, "Go find a pumpkin in the field
that you want to take home".

Many of the students picked a big pumpkin
like the one Suzie sings about
in her favorite song;
but I found a small one
that was just right for me.

Farm Fresh
quash
Apples

Soon the wagon took us back towards the farm.

There were so many fruits and vegetables, and we saw
a bee hive with busy buzzing bees making honey.

The farmer told us how important honeybees are
because they are pollinators.

This means the bees help by transferring pollen
(a fine powder) from one plant to another plant,
which is essential for all plants to have seeds,
flowers, fruits or vegetables.

Then the farmer gave us each a taste of the sweet delicious
honey that the bees make from sipping the flower's nectar.

He also told us that bees are just one type of pollinator.

 **Can you think of other pollinators
that are important for plants?** 

There was a maze made out of hay-bales,
and a huge hill of loose hay.

We all ran up to the top
and then rolled all the way to the bottom;
we even threw hay at each other.

Finally, we sat down on a bale of hay
to clean our hands and say a blessing before eating
the doughnuts that Suzie brought for our snack.

Another student gave everyone a drink
so our tummies were happy!

We took turns telling Mrs. B our favorite activity to do on the farm.

Janae`, Morgan and Dean said they really liked petting the animals.

Grey, Matt B. and Logan said they liked how smelly the farm was.

Matthew D., Zachary and Sam liked the bumpy ride.

Melissa, Mallory and Kendall liked jumping into the hay.

Kaitlin and Suzie like chasing the chickens and turkeys.

William and Matt M. liked rolling down the hill,
and I liked all of it, especially the bees!

Mrs. B told us how she would carve her pumpkin into
a jack-o-lantern and then take the seeds from the
pumpkin and roast them in the oven for us to eat.

This was a great day and I am so tired.

Now I can take a nap on the bus as it takes us back to school!

Colors
1 2 3 4 5 6 7 8 9 10
Humphrey's Journal
HUMPHREY

We arrived at school and Mrs. B read my journal to the class.

Everyone liked hearing about my time with Suzie.
The teacher told Suzie that she always makes people
feel special; she said it is a gift to be so kind.

Mrs. B said, "For homework we all should do
something kind for another person."

Then Mrs. B explained, "Some people might act mean because they
actually feel very sad inside. You can share a smile, a hug, a note with
a heart, or help someone clean up. Also playing with someone who
is alone or just giving a compliment can change someone's day!"

She said, "It would make us feel good too."

These students make me feel alive.
I love getting hugs; being kind is awesome!

What random acts of kindness could you do today?  

Who will be the next lucky student
to take me home?

See you soon for another
adventure in kindergarten.

Humphrey

Did you think about some of these pollinators?

Insects, birds, mammals, and lizards

some examples:
- bumble bees, wasps
- butterflies, moths
- lady bugs, flies, beetles, ants
- hummingbirds, many other birds
- lemurs, bats. squirrels, deer, and humans
- geckos, skinks
- the wind

About the Author

Terry Vail Blount — I grew up in Norfolk, Virginia, moved to nearby Virginia Beach where I raised two sons with my firefighter husband of fifty-two years. We are now proud grandparents of three awesome grandkids! I retired from teaching kindergarten and then pre-school a few years back; not a day has passed that I do not miss teaching children. I decided to use all of Humphrey's journals from my years of teaching to share with children and teachers about Humphrey's adventures in kindergarten. I could not have published this book without my illustrator Jeanne Munden, my talented long time friend.

About the Illustrator

Jeanne McGaha Munden grew up in Virginia and California due to her family's ties to the military. She's always enjoyed making art. She worked as a graphic designer and an art therapist and after retiring to Central Oregon, began illustrating Humphrey for books with her dear friend Terry Vail Blount. She is a proud Mom and Grandma and plans to spoil her grandchildren rotten.

www.ingramcontent.com/pod-product-compliance
Lightning Source LLC
Chambersburg PA
CBHW041646110726
48005CB00003B/728

9 798988 362920